The Mappila Verses

The Mappila Verses

Ajmal Khan A T

HAWAKAL

CALCUTTA | NEW DELHI

CALCUTTA | NEW DELHI

Hawakal Publishers

33/1/2 K B Sarani, Mall Road, Calcutta 80
70-B/9 Amritpuri, East of Kailash, New Delhi 65

Email info@hawakal.com
Website www.hawakal.com

First edition August, 2020

ISBN: 978-81-946651-8-2

Price: 300 INR | USD 9.99

for
my ancestors

ACKNOWLEDGEMENTS

I thank Jerry Pinto, Adil Jussawalla and Chandramohan S for reading these poems and for their kind words as blurb.

I thank Gafoor for helping me with Arabic, Paloma reading, and poets Meena Kandasamy, Arjun Rajendran, Shalim M. Hussain, Vivek Narayanan, K. Satchidanandan, Ashwani Kumar, Akhil Katyal, Ashraf Dali and Gábor Lanczkor for reading and guiding my poems at various points. I also thank Irshad, Aniket and Chitrangada for their constant support.

Thanks to Hawakal Publishers for publishing this.

CONTENTS

Portrait of a Bastard

Your collar bone protrudes like a Somalian Child
and the arm muscles anemic
but Lungi, from the Malabar Coast.

Texture of your skin is the mixture of Pulaya and
Cheruman
converted to Islam
sweat with a scent beyond Arabian sea from Dubai,
Abu Dhabi or Saudi Arabia.

How do you speak English this well?
You guys rebelled against them
and boycotted even their language.

How did you get this resilient yet deep eyes
and rage? somewhat remotely similar to Palestinians
and Kashmiris
You were never occupied.

Your chin remotely resembles
a clever north Indian Bania man
which disappear like a mirage.

They murmur, you are a bastard
in the confluence between the Arabian Coast
and the Malabar before Portuguese and Dutch
mastered maritime.

Do bastards have documents?
Of the unholy nights
Or they and their children and their children and their
children remain bastards forever?

Write me down, I am a Mappila

After Mahmoud Darwish in Palestine and Hafiz Ahmed in Assam

Write me down
I am a Mappila.
Write it down
My name is Ajmal.
I am a Muslim
And an Indian citizen
We are seven at home
And more is on the way
All are Indian by birth.
Do you want documents?

Write me down
That I am an Indian.
I am a Mappila
My ancestors were untouchables
Hindus in your language
Slapped on the face of Manu
They changed their names
When they were given dignity
Centuries ago
before forefathers of your ideologues were born.
Are you suspicious?

Write me down
I am a Mappila.
My ancestors tilled the soil here
They lived here
And died
Their roots are deeper than the roots of these Banyan
And Coconut trees
Though they weren't land lords
Only peasants
This land is their root.
The scent of their root is the scent of this land
The colour of their skin
Is the colour of this land
Do you want documents?

Write me down
I am a Mappila.
Do you still need documents?
Then I will dig the graves in Malabar
and many others
I want to show you the boots and bullets
On their chests
When they fell down with the British guns.
Do you still need documents?
I know what documents you have
The copy of a confession in Cellular jail and
The blood stains of Gandhi on your hand
Do you want me to remind you of more stains?
I say
Shut the fuck up
If you ask me for documents.

Write me down
I am a Mappila.
Remember
I have not forgotten

You sent people to demolish Masjid
But now
You have demolished the constitution
The soul of this land.
I am angry
How dare you?
How dare you?

Write me down
I am a Mappila.
This is my land
If I have born here
I will die here.
Therefor
Write it down
Clearly
In bold and capital letters
On the top of your NRC
That I am an Indian.

Biriyani

She says, she likes Biryani like a child longing for chocolates.
I asked her with the menu I have
which one she likes.
Hyderabadi, Mughlai, Malabari, Moradabadi
Calcutta Biriyani, Lucknowi Biriyani
Tehri Biriyani or Thalasheri Biriyani.
Kozhi Biriyani and Kampuri Biryani.
Beary Biriyani, Bombay Biriyani and Bihari Biryani
Dindigul Biriyani or Bhatkal Biriyani
Kachi Biriyani and Ambur Biriyani.
Like a child denied the favorite chocolate on the menu
She told me, *Veg Biriyani*!
Further, I didn't ask about the Kashmiri Biriyani.

The word *Biriyani* is also used as slur for Muslims in some parts of India.

Rejected Poem

The poem was accused
as anti-national
and rejected
like a US visa applicant
from a Muslim country.
It wanted to prove as nationalist
It started with Vande Matharam
The continuing lines were only nouns
of the independence struggles
in which the poem was part of
Rest of the lines were written in Green
White and Kesari in color.
Signed on the lines which start with J&K
that they are the integral part
it ended with national anthem.
The poem was rejected again
on the grounds
It had two names Hyder Ali and Tipu Sultan
in the footnote
Syntax had no saffron and khaki pattern
Moplah rebellion is included as one line
And instead of 1947
its written *Azaadi*.

9 Ways to Look at a Cow in India

1. Did the Hindus never ate beef?
Dr. Ambedkar said yes
they did.

2. Cow is a holy animal – said the Brahmin
and waited for Dalit
to remove the dead cow.

3. "The cow and the bull are sacred
and therefore, should be eaten" –
Apastamba Dharma Sutra.

4. Aklaq didn't eat it –
the postmortem report
and forensic report.

5. There are only Muslims and Dalits or Adivasi killed
in the race of Gau Raksha
why?

6. Urine and cow dung
the holy profit sometimes
than the milk.

7. Who got the profit of cow?
Mosalman butcher? The Baniya exporter?
or the Saffron?

8. Again, one more killed
was told, he ate beef
No one asked
if he had food to eat.

Gulbarg Society

A black cat is still hanging around here and there
for many years now
since 2002.
The old blood scars have become black
like the colour of the cat skin.
Spiders have made nets
that covered many scars.
Pigeons have made nests on the chimney
that was burned.
There is silence everywhere
a dead silence
the silence coming out of the fear of danger
The colour of the fear is the colour of the burned kids dress
when they were burned alive.
The word truth is capable to shake the founding
stones of the building.
The dusty case files in the Supreme court and High court
have become food for termites.
The wind that use to come sometimes from the East
and embrace the building says
"wait, the truths will come out one day
you have to wait until justice come"
It has been long since the wind came
Its scared of the cat, spiders or termites?

Peace be upon You in Delhi Metro

It's around 10 am in Dubai.
After a couple of months silent break
He calls me before his first shift
As-salamu Alaykum...
As-salamu Alaykum...
Silence this side
Pause, hello...
Hello... hello
Assalamu Alaikum...
Pause
Again, silence... and in a broken tone... *How are you?*
From this side
The uneasy *I am fine* came after five seconds of silence
that lasted like 5 five hours.
In the background
Any unattended or suspicious articles like briefcase, bag, toy,
thermos or transistor, etc. could be bomb.
After a long broken in between conversation
My metro stops at Jahangir Puri in the Yellow line.
Door will open on the right
Please mind the gap.
I am still caught in the unsaid Wa alaykumu s-salam.
Two days ago, there was a bomb blast in Delhi.

Yesterday when I went out, I didn't consciously wear a Kurta
I have been telling my friends
If we are in crowds, railway station, bus, metro, streets
Call me by my nick name.
He complained to my mother
I am becoming non-religious and
I take my connecting bus outside the metro station.

Papyrus Citizen

The tree they made paper out of
Stood in front of the citizens tribunal verification
Like an illegal immigrant – to verify the papers of its legal status.

On the Way Back

Staring at stars, cosmos and beyond
We went to colleges and universities
like curious children following constellations.
Some of us – the only one of our kind
The rest had something similar – their surnames, parent's jobs
Or the names of the cities they hailed
The kind of dress they wore, the way they spoke English
The brands of cigarettes they smoked and the scent of their sweat.
Some dropped out
Few missing
Others came home as dead bodies like – Shambuka
Those survived were picked up and
the remaining – untouchables in the job market.
On the way back to the village
The road is long with the heavy burden of degree certificates.

Why don't you forget a Mosque?
An old building made by someone is that important?

It wasn't a Mosque

The
pillars
that
held
my
courage

The walls I carried my identity

The domes   this country declared sEc*U*lar- remains

B

R

0

K

E   N.

My Ride to Bandra

We had just passed Kurla west
They have so many children you know
Driving in the Bombay traffic from Sion
To break the lasting silence from Chembur, he said
That is why so much traffic here
And they live so dirty
Uneducated, Illiterates
The adjectives – my guide to understand
Who he was talking about, or do I need them?
My embarrassed smile and the silent responses
were agreement for him.
He asks if I know after the last bomb blast
Someone was picked up from here.
Looking at me, confused if I was deaf
He concludes, he doesn't know how *these* people can
become terrorists easily
and stopped his one-way conversation.
The traffic had moved and we were reaching Bandra
The breezy welcome from the sea couldn't inform me we had reache
Sir, we have arrived.
On the Taxi App of his phone
my name appeared in big and bold capital letters
its 450 rupees
I smiled at him with a smileless smile.
His phone rang
Hiding his left face with the phone, he said
Hello Sir, *I just completed a trip and coming soon.*
My *trip* continued.

Do You Ask Identity Cards to Birds?

They belong to sky
Sky belongs to them
Wings – their identity card
Like the colour of my skin – this land
Not the skin that feels brown only when it crosses the sea.

Surviving Here

Not for your sake, but
mine, at airports and on planes
I act extra nice.

(Being Arab, Hayan Charara)

Clean shaved like Sahara
I avoid Kurta-Paijama
My accent and diet.
I chant – *I am not a Pakistani or Bangladeshi* like Zikr.
I take extra care to hide my name and
Look around carefully
Before I reply – *and peace be upon you too.*
Have you ever made peace with what you are not?
I do –
for peace's sake.

Where Do We Go?

Where should we go after the last frontiers?
Where should the birds fly after the last sky?
Where should the plants sleep after the last breath of air?
Mahmoud Darwish

After the Isha Namaz
Chanting prayers sitting in her Musalla
Keeping her copy of Quran aside with the Thasbeeh, she asks
Where do we go if our names are not in the list?

Where do coconut trees go
when their roots are declared illegal?
How does Hibiscus flower if you ask them
go back where they come from?
Can you ask Tapioca to go back to Brazil?
Do you ask tea and coffee to go back where they come from?
Where do Great Pied Hornbills go
when you tell monsoons are illegal to them?
Where do Mackerels and Sardines go
when you inform them, they are illegal in the water?
Do Malabar elephant have identity card to enter the Maasai Mara?
Where do Lion-tailed macaque go if they are asked to
vacate the Silent Valley?

Can *Mundakan* and *Puncha* paddy be cultivated in Saudi Arabia?
Which water Giant Danio's swim if rivers are made illegal to them?
Is there a list of snakes that are allowed only on the Western Ghats?
On which seas Hassinar fish if you ask him
documents to enter the Arabian sea?

Where do we go?
The sword breaks my silence, she asks again
Where?
I reminded

"For your father, Adam
was created with dirt from the surface of the earth.
You also will be returned to
the earth"
We came from soil
We go to soil, until then
We live here.

Ghèto

After 1947
where we lived became another country.
A country within a country – mini-Pakistan
our gullies – until the *final solution*.

Indian First or Muslim?

My mother read Quran
Much like Imams in Mecca and Madeena.
Her mother recites Mappila Ramayanam in Karkidakam
better than Karthyayani's Kilippattu.
Bob Marley ignites me like Kabir Kala Manch.
My brother's earphone is louder
with Michael Jackson and Shakira.
My niece picks up Hum Dekhenge from her compulsory Hindi class
I dream in Malayalam and
write poems in English
though our ancestors led war against Robert Hitchcock.
My colonized rhythm and postcolonial syntax – confused
If you are Hindu first or Indian
Or they – synonyms.

Emigration Counter After 9/11

His eyes were caught on two things
My name and
My domicile – Malappuram.
My colorful boarding pass
United Airways to New York.
I- Clean shaved – the only few hairs
Like early pubic hair
In T-shirt and Jeans
The days I wore a skull cap is not near the memory.
Hope – he doesn't ask me to open the underwear.
Looking at me and the computer screen again and again
He said,
You have to wait until my higher officer comes and
verifies that you are not a terrorist.
I remind as an inconvenience – to those behind me in the line
For being me.

Pehlu Khan

The fault was – name
and born – here
Like your name – during frisking
And a Muslim – in India
Or a black like – George Floyd
But *No Lives Matter*
Some lives aren't lives.

Shaheen Bagh

Mothers and sisters came with Azaadi on dupattas
And Inquilab on their hijabs
To give crash course on constitution after Babasaheb.

As the caravan of double marginalized got together
Feminism arrived to protect and claim
Like momentary clouds over the Delhi sky during
monsoons.

On an evening, after the sun set
A Khadi prays
Oh god, let this women's fight not go in vain
Like Amina's.
From 85-year-old
To 3-year-old declare together
They will fight until their last breath
Destiney of a Muslim after 73 long years.

On an unsettled evening
Another crowd appear with saffron flags and shout
Desh ke gaddaron ko Goli maro saalon ko
And an English news anchor shouts
Your message has been conveyed, now please go homes

Home? – Whose?
We get massacred on roads in the broad daylight
And then on TV channels and newspapers.

On another evening gathering, a poet sings
Martyrs are not dead
They live with us
Image of Bhagat Sigh kept on the backyard smiles.

Do Not cause inconvenience to public – Wisdom of justice
Unlike other times, they are not a delay at the security check
Their existence – an inconvenience.

On the republic day flag was hoisted
With the hands of another mother
Accompanied by more than those who assembled at Rajpath
A republic is reclaimed in the same city at the same time
A new country is born in the imagination
Until document verification.

National List of Micro Aggressions (Incomplete)

1. *Do you eat pork?*
2. *You must have got terrorist training in Madrasa. Haven't you?*
3. *Why do you guys keep a beard? just shave it man!*
4. *Why do you keep on saying your religion is of peace? it would have shown up, if it was!*
5. *You have a pet? Aren't dogs haram?*
6. *You guys marry many!*
7. *Salle Mulle!*
8. *So, do you also support Jihadis?*
9. *Why don't you condemn Taliban/ ISIS?*
10. *I don't mean anything, but why all terrorists are Muslims?*
11. *Is condom Haram?*
12. *Your mother tongue must be Urdu, right?*
13. *Do you have all documents? Keep all of them ready and safe okay. Let's see!*
14. *Hey, I haven't said your name to my parents yet okay. My family doesn't like me to have Muslim friends.*
15. *How do you guys eat cow man?*
16. *Do you have roots in Bangladesh?*
17. *But you don't look like a Muslim!*

18. *You guys are violent!*
19. *I have heard you guys don't use condoms? Is that why you are so many?*
20. *Does your mother wear a burqa?*
21. *But why so many of you are in Jails? All of them can't be innocent right?*
22. *Look, you people get angry very fast!*
23. *I have heard you guys can have up to four women, Kya Maza Hain Yaar?*
24. *Fuck you, Go to Pakistan!*
25. *You feel Indian first or Muslim?*
26. *How do you speak English this well?*
27. *Are you supporting India or Pakistan today?*
28. *What stops you from saying Vande Mataram?*
29. *But you are a Muslim!*
30. *So, is it more pleasurable to have a circumcised one? I mean...*
31. *You must be having so many children at home?*
32. *When I say my name is – Ohh Ajmal Kasab?*
33. *You might be supporting Triple Talaq, don't you?*
34. *This place is a Mini-Pakistan.*
35. *You must be supporting separatists in Kashmir!*

Martyrs
after Khalil Gibran

When those who
martyred waging war
don't live in your poems,
they say,
You and your poems
are party to their death
and died forever.

Love

We looked at each other's eyes
Caught in each other's and
Found a new world.
Our two different worlds became one
Hearts, souls and bodies
Until suddenly asked,
What is your name?
When I said, *my name is...*
They said
Love Jihad.

Mappila Verse

This is the song the old bearded
Auliya sang long long ago
The song depicting the Ramayanam story
We wait to hear in every Karkidkam.

Mappila Muslim Ramayanam

Ram's place of birth – Babar's Masjid
Babar's Masjid – Ram's place of birth
Ram and Masjid
Masjid and Ram
Ram's Nikah – Sita
Vappa – Dasharathan
Ravana – Sultan of Lanka
Valmiki – Long bearded Auliya
Like my Arabi-Malayalam
That couldn't differentiate between an Arabi and a Malayali.

Not Your Mia

"I am not your Nigro"
"The history of America is the history of the Negro in
America
And it's not a pretty picture."

James Baldwin

We were chopped into two in 1947 by an English man
And the wounds still bleed
Sometimes heavy and other – steady.

They wiped the blood with blood – on both sides
As more than a million-blood dropped – many
disappeared.

1964 – the city of joy sleep with horror
Of the dead bodies and the wounded.

Eid prayers at Moradabad in 1980
Unknown numbers – bodies
Known names – mass graves.

Babar Ki Aulado Ko, Bhago Pakistan Ya Khabaristan
Echoed at Bhagalpur – 1980
Kabristan was flooded with bodies in Kafan.

Nellie is the name of the memory of 1983
For the 2000 and more
That got erased between the border with Bangladesh.

1987 is written with the Kafan in Hashimpura
We thought those letters will fade like a thunder
lightning
Thunder still echoes – increasing everyday like early
monsoon.

1990 the yatra on Rath for Ram
Ramlala Hum Layenge Mandir Wahi Banayenge.

Bombay should have less Landya to be cosmopolitan
Hence, 1990 and 91
And from that ashes Shiva's avatar takes birth and –
Mumbra.

The flames reached Hyderabad
Many more went to Jannat and Jahannam.

If Gujarat is the model from 2002
Either face or the mirror needs to be changed
Or my head – to be chopped off
I am trying hard to forget Gujarat.

Muzaffar Nagar still weeps in crisis
Like lost children – of those who are alive
Rest weeps from haven as rain.

The Indian flag hoisted at Shaheen Bagh and the
Preamble of constitution in 2020 Delhi
Desh Ke Gaddaron Ko, Goli Maro Saalon Ko in the
background.

The pretty picture has scars – where there is Mia
Like deep bullet marks on a big banner
Sachar commission report – the holy text after Quran
Waiting to be chopped off from the list
As D-voter or D-citizen
From the midnight to no sunrise
I stand looking at my own pretty picture between the
search for documents.

Termites

Around 150 million years ago they – stared to
decompose
They ate the Inca, Egyptians, and Romans
Harappa and Mohan Jadaro.
We need to check termites entering home
They are infiltrators to our soil – He declares on TV
The law of nature hanged like a sword on his neck
They have already eaten his ancestors' dead bodies and
Will eat his descendants.

When Covid-19 Came for Us

Corona took off from Wuhan, flew to America
And arrived as a Chinese virus like a Chinese emigrant.
In between had transit in Milan
Where it was known as The Asian virus
Further somewhere in between had easy connections to Africa
South America, Australia and beyond known as
Covid-19 or The Wuhan virus.
No immigration counters could stop the illegal immigrant.
Unlike other Chinese products
Unwelcomed around the world
It came for us.
Before it reached my country – they say
It went to shut the Mecca and Vatican City
And via Nizamudin it spread here
It then altered my Manipuri friend's name into Chinese virus
Before camouflaged as Corona Jihad.

Name

My name is an Arabic word like thousand others
Why don't you guys have Indian names? – She
Like a question posed during the citizen's verification.
Looking at my left corner of the left eye
She asks – what does it mean?
It means you! I answer
Our world become one with an Arabic name and an Indian
What does it mean? she flirts again
It means you
It means you, the most beautiful
I said
She didn't get it – that conversation ended
Another sun sets in the West.

My Spelling Mistakes – Mappila English

My native tongue continues to struggle against the imperialism
It has not come in terms with the independence
Its accent echoes my ancestors
Grammar – Shurda mixture
Syntax's cosmology – tribal
Rhymes are a confluence of Malayalam and Arabic
Arabi – Malayalam.
My language and the spelling mistakes – the last proofs
That I have not yet defeated
Like a soldier yet to be killed.

لغة هذه الأيام

من خلق هذا الخوف من المجهول؟
مثل الخوف من لغتي
كيف أصبحت لغتي غريبة عليك
عندما أكون أخاك؟
لماذا أنت خائف مني ولغتي
عندما أكون جارك؟
كيف أصبحت إرهابيا حتى أثبت برائتي؟

Language these Days

Who created this fear of the unknown?
Like the fear of my language
How did my language become alien to you
When I am your brother?
Why are you scared of me and my language
When I am your neighbour?
How did I become a terrorist until proven innocent?

Native Son and Motherland

My mother
My own mother asks for my documents
Like a foreigner arrived at the port of entry
I look for documents
My document – umbilical cord
Her colour – my skin
Her blood – my veins
Her black mole – my birth mark
Her long hair – my trimmed
Her vagina – echo of my first cry
She – suspicious
Do all mothers ask for documents from their own
children?
My mother – suspicious of my birth
Our names are mixed with Arabic letters along with
Malayalam
She looks at the grown beard – the way I speak
She looks at my menu card
She asks me to open my pant zip
Do all mothers ask for documents from their own
children?
Like my motherland.

Kaka

a Malayalam song

Hey Crow where is your nest?
Is there a little crow in the nest?
If you do not give food to the little one
will the little crow be crying?

(Malayalam poem)

Kaka is black in colour and not – the bird of colour
It's uninvited like a bad omen and
then invited to eat the leftover – after cremation.
Eat the beloved chick – clean the litter and
eat the shit.
The hated Kaka – they say
are intelligent and smart
unlike human beings they even survived multiple extinctions and
not vegetarian by birth.
Cuckoo's come to lay eggs on their nests
– still hated.

Kaka in Malayalam is crow and also a slur used for Muslims.

How do I become illegal,
unlike the plants
birds
butterflies
animals and
fish,
when I am one among them?

My Non-Poetry

My poetry is not listed in the NRC
Like a Mia from Goalpara
It is accused of not carrying Indian poetics –
carrying foreign images.
They examined its syntax and said
Its origin – from the tribals in Arabia
My poems have migrant Arabic letters mixed with
Malayalam like Arabi-Malayalam.

Mappila Verse

The first step in liquidating a people is to erase its memory. Destroy its books, its culture, its history. Then have somebody write new books, manufacture a new culture, invent a new history. Before long that nation will begin to forget what it is and what it was... The struggle of man against power is the struggle of memory against forgetting.
Milan Kundera

Centuries ago
Even before Baba Sahib was born
My ancestors search for caste annihilation – they
became Mappila.

Malik Dinar came to my coast with light
Cheraman Perumal – lit Diya
Cheramaan Juma Mosque – first masjid on the
subcontinent
Two lights merged between the Mecca and Ponnani.

Quadi Muhammed weaved songs when Portuguese
arrived
Like Cannons on my disposal
Before anyone know anything about songs of resistance
on my coast.

Kunjali Marakkar, Variyankunnath and Ali Musliyar
Might sound just Muslim names for you
– the light houses of self-respect and freedom for my land.

The brave children of Eranadu and Valluvanadu who poured their blood
The land that showed chest to the cannons in 1921
The brave children of Eranadu and Valluvanadu who poured their blood
The land that showed chest to cannons in 1921 – My lullaby

Anglo-Mappila war – My bedtime stories
When my ancestors fought against the sons of the empire
On which the sun never set
On another sunset Wagon massacre paintings
were removed from Tirur railway station
How do you remove the wounds?

This land is built with the blood of my ancestors
The water we drink – their sweat
Their blood on my nerve
You – stand stable on their dead bodies.

Overnight,
I have become orphan at my own home
Or it wasn't – home?
I now dig names graves and blood stains
Of my people to get all of us free – certificates of loyalty
I stand alone at the Ghat of this country
With all the documents and history
For my citizenship approval.

Malabari Landya in North India

Miyavu Miyavu – the kitten
Miyavu started to break between Miya and vu –
Then only Miya...Miya...became clear
Oh Miya..!
It took some time to accommodate the new Mia tale on
my name
I carried it like the major differences between
Hominoidea and
Homo Sapiens.
Katua.. Katua.. Katu – ua Kat – ua
Yes, they were calling Katua
It took some research to understand what does it mean
It felt like I got circumcised once again.
In the unsettled evening
On the dining table
He said
Ha Landya Dukarache maans khat nahi
No, this Landay doesn't eat Pork.
They called my friend Vivek
– Mr. Vivek, Vikek and
Vikek Nair or Mr. Nair.

Our House Hunt

We had lost the count of houses we visited
We could only look for the once
That were on the bottom of the lists
I went back and forth thinking of my fellowship amount
And the rent
This must have been the 25th or 26th one
They said it's a cozy 2 bhk
And fully furnished
Gated society
No restrictions, chilled out and liberal landlords
Kya naam hain aapka?
My friend told his
Aur aapka?
I said mine
She said, *sorry.*

Untitled

After we get the best Mutton Rogan Josh in Bombay – dinner
He would still say 'it's never like the Rogan Josh at home!'
He sleeps before I finish my late-night affairs
Between 2.am and 5.am before Azan
He makes this disturbing sounds in sleep
Mostly in his mother tongue and sometimes in English
Our room become the downtown Srinagar on Friday
I could only recognize Curfew,
Azaadi and sometimes PhD all this while.
During summer breaks
He went home and we never spoke over phone
He didn't get a Bombay number and his other number
Mostly unreachable or remain out of coverage.
I wait for his arrival from Srinagar
Like how Bombay wait for monsoons by the end of May
I wait, in fact for the apples he carries along
He claims, they are the best in the world
From that night
I could only hear he crying and crawling in sleep and
His silence by the day.
After few weeks he went home and then
We met only in dreams
Thereafter my other roommate started asking,
You started talking while you were asleep
Is everything fine?

Hindu Khatre Mein Hain

Mohammed Akhlaq – lynched in the broad daylight and
Tabrez Ansari and Hafiz Junaid
Their names – look – tongue – to be killed
Hindu Khatre Mein Hai.

Bilal was picked up and his mother doesn't know
His whereabouts since last 25 years
Yes – 25 years
His basti's synonym – Mini-Pakistan
Hindu Khatre Mein Hai.

8-year-old Asifa, 8 – year – old girl, Asifa
Was brutally raped and murdered
A bud was cut before it was bloomed
Hindu Khatre Mein Hai.

Najeeb Ahmed is still missing – his mother keeps asking
Where is Najeeb?
Where is Najeeb?
Where is Najeeb?
Hindu Khatre Mein Hai.

NRC was passed and
Termites will be checked
Hindu Khatre Mein Hai
Hindu Khatre Mein Hai.

Writing

One cannot write poems about trees when the forest is
full of police.

Bertolt Brecht

Birds, sky and villages
Clouds, river and fishes
Hills, dew and forests
Malgudi days, Aymenam and Mussoorie flashes
Like afternoon drams and I sit to write.

News flashes
Bomb blast in Mumbai-30 killed
My phone rings incessantly – Mother
On the other side
Text appears from brother
Are you safe? – From the attack and the aftermath
My dream world finished like an incomplete film before
climax
I close myself – to the world and to self.

I sit to write again
This is not what I wanted to write
This is what I could.

Non-Chameleon

Aurangzeb road – to Nizamuddin
And to Allahabad
Dr. APJ Abdul Kalam road – to Nizamuddin
For my train to Prayagraj.
Names – unlike chameleon's colour
Change permanently
Oshiwara station as Ram Mandir
Mughalsarai Junction – Pandit Deen Dayal
Upadhyaya Nagar
Taj Mahal – Tejo Mahalaya.
What happens when you change your names – conversion
Unlike my ancestors
I wait for *ghar wapsi* into a non-existing *ghar*.

Mappila Verse – English Mala

Variyankunnathu Mala
Bismillah al-Rahman al-Rahim
For *Variyankunnathu Kunjahammed Haji*

Let this begin with Bismi Hamdh and Swalath
Remembering Muhyadheen Mala
Qadi Muhammed
Nafeesath Mala – Other Malas and Sufis.

This is about the one – Born to Chakkiparamban
Moideen and
Paraveeti Kunjaisha in Nellikutu.

The one – His father Moideen fought the British and
The son upheld his legacy.

The one – Short – with a Malabar brown complexion in
a red cap and
An artist who played *Kolkali* and *Duffmuttu*.

The one – Wrote our names in the golden letters
Fighting the whites which we have forgotten.

The one – Gave his life

For this land and is shining like a star above us.

The one – Shaheed upholding this land and
We became Aazaad from the whites.

The one – Poured his blood
On that strength we stood for last 100 years.

You Variyamkunnat, You Shaheed Variyamkunnat
I weave this Mala to.

*

In the history answer sheet
I wrote your name instead of 1921.

Tilka Maanji, Bhima Koregaon, Malabar-war
Freedom struggles – not in my history text books.

On my wall
You are between Ambedkar and Birsa Munda.

"The brave Variyamkunnat prepared Mappilas to fight
The brave warrior prepared Mappilas fight the British" -
My lullaby.

Your name – address to Eranadu, Valluvanadu and
Ponnani
Your fame – name to Malabar, Malayalam Nadu and
India.

The brave children of Eranadu who poured the blood
The land that showed chest to the British Cannons –
Sings the poet.

The paddy we harvest will not be allowed to feed the
landlords
And our money will not be allowed to send London –
Slogans of your struggle.

Andaman, Bombay and Mecca – Your exiles
Eranadu, Valluvanadu and Malayalanadu – Your home
land.

You – The symbol of anti-colonial struggle and the star
of secularism
You – The hero for anti-feudal struggles by the
depressed classes.

You – The learned Mappila of the 19th century
Wrote letters in the language of the enemy.

"History is written by the winner, defeated the bad ones
in the story" –
The caution I got when searching for you in the history.

In that history – Mappila is fanatic, Wagon massacre –
Wagon tragedy
Malabar freedom struggle – Mappila Rebellion
To the same history – The first war of independence –
Sepoy Mutiny.

You were gunned down by the sons of the empire on
which the sun never set
You then – Shaheed Variyamkunnat.

You were offered holy Mecca to live forever but
You said *I will die fighting for this land and that is
holiest* – Hubbul Watani Minal Imaan.

We have no hate to Hindus, we won't spare the once
who support British
And your name for that country – Malayalam Nadu.

"In the name of god, I will give my life to the India
That Gandhi and Maulana want" – your words that
You kept.

You – The brave Mappila son who fought for all the
depressed classes and
You – The flame of hope for Shudras.

For Mappilas you were what Omar al-Mukhtar for
Libyans
Messali Hadj for Algerians and Mandela to South
Africans.

You – The most dangerous man of Malabar
For the British.

You – The only brave son of the subcontinent
established self-rule
under the nose of The Empire.

Your peasant organizing and struggles
Echoed in Russia to Lenin and Mao in China.

Your each beard was being pulled out, you were
denailed
And you were bleeding
*Don't Shoot me from behind, let me look at this land and
Looking at this land let me fall apart* – your last brave
words.

When you were shot and falling to your motherland as
you wished

Your enemy shouts *What a brave Mappila leader.*

You were killed like Che Guevara and
They did to you what they did to Che Guevara after
your martyrdom.

Years of my search for your portrait ended with –
They even destroyed all his pictures.

You marked yourself as the king of Hindus, Ameer to
Mohammadens
And the Colonel of Khilafat movement.

Those who called you communal don't know the names
of your enemies –
Khan Bahadur Chekutti, Kondotty Thangal and other
British allied Mappilas
They don't know that your army had more Hindus.

You – The son of this land
You – The gift of this land
You – The soldier of this land
You – The pride of this land.

You – The flame of hope in the darkness spread by the
British in Malabar
You – The one who led war in Pookkottur and Manjeri.

You – The revolutionary of the 19th century India and
Brave fighter of the Malayalam Land.

The one who dreamed for a self-rule – self respect
The one who dreamed of a mother land without British.

The one who took arm against the British and landlords
with the same hands

The one who united Hindus and Muslims in the same
army.

You –The bullock cart driver turned freedom fighter
and
Then martyr.

After 100 years – descendance of the one who killed
Gandhi and
The grandsons of the one who wrote confession at
Cellular – examiners
Of your loyalty to the mother land.

The one who don't even have a child in the history to
represent
Examine your love for this land.

You – The one who gave identity to Mappila
Standing at the forefront.

You – The one on whose courage we stand tall
And proud.

You and your struggles
The brave chapters of the Indian freedom struggle.

*Writing poetry for the benefit of knowledge is equal to
worship of god*
Says – Fath al Mubin, Quadi Muhammed in Calicut.

This humble me of the same land
Privilege to write this
You ignite us and I pay respect to you brave Variyam.

The literal meaning of Mala is chain in Malayalam. The Mala genre of Mappila songs are generally written in Arabic-Malayalam script are praises of pious personalities of Islam who were supposed to have gained high spiritual status. These songs narrate the superhuman deeds of the saints. Each Mala initially corresponded to the leader of a Sufi order called *Thareequath* who was abundantly showered praises in the poetry, often well-exceeding the limits of human capabilities. Popular among these are the *Muhyidheen Mala* the *Rifa'i mala*, the *Shaduli Mala*, the *Ajmeer Mala*, and the *Nafeesath Mala*. Each of these corresponded to their respective Sufi orders while the last is about *Nafeesathul Misriyya*, a woman Sufi saint of Egypt more commonly known as Sayyida Nafeesa. There are hundreds of Mala songs written like this in Kerala. Later Mala songs were also started being written on other prominent people such as legendary Malayalam writer Vaikom Muhmmad Basheer, called *Basheer Mala* and on Dalit leader Iyyankali, called *Iyyankali Mala*.

Variyankunnathu Kunjahammed Haji was one of the prominent leaders of the anti-colonial struggle in Malabar. He seized control of a large area from the British and established an Independed Malayalam Land called Malayalamnaadu and run a parallel government in open defiance of the British rule. He was captured and executed by the British in 1921 and his dead body was burned without leaving any trace as the British didn't wanted his legacy to be known. This is the first Mala poem ever written in English and the first Mala about Variyankunnathu.